FOLENS PHOTOPACK TUDOR MONARCHS

Steve Harrison

INTRODUCTION

First published 1995 by Folens Limited.
United Kingdom: Folens Publishers,
Apex Business Centre, Boscombe Road,
Dunstable, LU5 4RL.
Email: folens@folens.com

Ireland: Folens Publishers, Greenhills
Road, Tallaght, Dublin 24.
Email: info@folens.ie

Poland: JUKA, ul. Renesansowa 38,
Warsaw 01-905.

Editor: Ian Jenkins
Layout artist: Pat Hollingsworth
Illustrations: Tony O'Donnell – Graham-
Cameron Illustration
Cover image: © Belvoir Castle,
Leicestershire/Bridgeman Art Library,
London
Cover design: In Touch Creative Services
Ltd.

The author and publisher would like to
thank the following for permission to
reproduce photographs:
Photo 1 (Henry VII) by courtesy of the
National Portrait Gallery, London.
Photo 2 (Henry VIII) © Belvoir Castle,
Leicestershire/Bridgeman Art Library,
London.
Photo 3 (Hampton Court) © Zefa
Pictures.
**Photo 4 (The Field of the Cloth of
Gold)** The Royal Collection © Her
Majesty the Queen.
Photo 5 (Family of Henry VIII)
The Royal Collection © Her Majesty the
Queen.
Photo 6 (Edward VI) by courtesy of the
National Portrait Gallery, London.
Photo 7 (Lady Jane Grey) © Victoria
and Albert Museum, London/Bridgeman
Art Library, London.
Photo 8 (Mary Tudor) © Prado,
Madrid/Scala, Florence.
**Photo 9 (Elizabeth 1 Armada
Portrait)** © Private Collection/
Bridgeman Art Library, London.
**Photo 10 (Execution of Mary Queen
of Scots)** © Scottish National Portrait
Gallery.
**A2 poster (detail from The Field of
the Cloth of Gold)** The Royal Collection
© Her Majesty the Queen.

© 1995 Folens Limited, on behalf of the
author.

Every effort has been made to trace the
copyright holders of material used in this
publication. If any copyright holder has
been overlooked, we should be pleased
to make any necessary arrangements.

British Library Cataloguing in
Publication Data. A catalogue record for
this publication is available from the
British Library.

ISBN 1 85276 694-8

The Tudor Age began in 1485 when the last of the Plantagenet kings, Richard III, was defeated and killed at Bosworth Field, near Leicester. Henry Tudor and the House of Lancaster had triumphed over the Yorkists. The Wars of the Roses were at an end and England had a new monarch and a new dynasty. Henry VII was the first of the Tudor monarchs.

The Tudor Age ended in 1603 with the death of Elizabeth I. In practice it spanned only three generations: Henry VII, Henry VIII and his three children – Mary, Elizabeth and Edward. Also included in this *Photopack* are Lady Jane Grey and Mary Queen of Scots, both of whom had claims as Tudor monarchs advanced on their behalf.

In helping children understand the events of the past it is important that they have a grasp of the context in which those events took place.

Children today will be conversant with the notion of a 'love' marriage in western culture and 'arranged' marriages in some other cultures, but they may not have an understanding of 'political' marriages. The prospective spouse of a European monarch in Tudor times was judged on the basis of political alliances, the balance of power and the Catholic and Protestant developments taking place at the time.

The photos have not been numbered or labelled in order to allow the children to use visual clues to infer who is featured. This will facilitate activities such as using deduction to place the photographs in chronological order, or placing them in the form of a family tree. Each page in this book contains background information, a fact file, key questions and ideas for activities. The copiable activity sheets provide a range of extension activities.

PHOTOPACK – *Tudor Monarchs*

© Folens

HENRY VII

Henry VII's reign was marked by peace, in contrast to the Wars of the Roses. He exercised close control over government and died a wealthy monarch. He did not pursue expensive foreign wars. Part of his legacy is the Henry VII Chapel in Westminster Abbey, one of the finest chapels ever constructed.

Henry's wife, Elizabeth of York, died in 1503. As a powerful European monarch, Henry considered marrying again as part of a political alliance. This portrait was commissioned by Margaret of Austria, daughter of the Emperor Maximillian I. She was considering marriage to Henry and wanted a realistic portrait. The rose represents not only the House of Tudor, but also love. Henry had been awarded the Order of the Golden Fleece by Maximillian, which he wears in the portrait. Apparently, Margaret was not impressed and the marriage did not take place!

Key questions

1. Who is this king? How do we know?
2. What is he holding in his right hand? What does this symbolise?
3. When was the portrait painted?
4. Henry was born in 1457. How old was he when this portrait was painted?
5. Is this a flattering portrait? How could it have been made more flattering?
6. Why might he have wanted his portrait painted looking through a window?

Fact file

Parents	Edmund Tudor and Margaret Beaufort
Born	1457 at Pembroke Castle
Reigned	1485 to 1509
Married	Elizabeth of York
Children	Arthur, Henry VIII, Margaret, Mary
Died	1509
Buried	Westminster Abbey

Activities

- Comparisons could be made between Henry VII's dress and appearance and those of his son, Henry VIII. The children could complete a chart, like the one below.

Feature	Henry VII	Henry VIII
Build		
Eye colour		
Hairstyle		
Facial hair		
Head wear		
Ornament		

The red rose represented both the House of Tudor and love.

- Ask the children to write a description of Henry's dress and appearance. They could focus on clothes, hair, ornaments, facial hair and expression.

HENRY VIII

© Belvoir Castle, Leicestershire / Bridgeman Art Library, London

Henry VIII was the second son of Henry VII. His elder brother, Arthur, was heir to the throne and in early life Henry was prepared for the traditional role of the second son, which would not have involved leading the country. In 1501 Arthur (aged 15) married Catherine of Aragon (aged 17), daughter of Ferdinand and Isabella of Spain. Within six months Arthur was dead.

Henry VII thought the alliance between England and Spain was so important that he obtained a dispensation from Pope Julius II, allowing Catherine to be betrothed to the 11-year-old Henry. The marriage could have taken place when Henry was 14, but by then Henry VII was less keen on the Spanish alliance. Young Henry was 18 years old when his father died in 1509. He then chose to marry Catherine.

Henry VIII is popularly remembered for his six wives and numerous affairs. However, his reign was characterised by involvement in foreign wars, all of which cost money and most of which were unsuccessful. As a consequence Henry needed more and more finance.

Activities

- Ask the children to paint two pictures. These could be pictures of themselves, a friend or the teacher. The first should be how the painter sees the other person and the second how the other person wishes to be depicted. Think about pose, dress location, expression.
- Ask the children to bring to school photos of themselves and their families. These should be both casual snaps and (if possible) studio-posed photos taken on special occasions, including school photos. They could compare them in a chart, like the one shown below.

Details	Posed	Snaps
Clothes		
Hair		
Smartness		
Surroundings		
Direction of eyes		
Purpose		
Any special preparation		

Key questions

1. How has the artist shown Henry's wealth?
2. Does Henry look a strong and powerful king? How?
3. What does the portrait tell us about his home?
4. What materials were used to make his clothes?
5. Would Henry have worn clothes like this every day? Explain.
6. Henry was described as 'having a healthy appetite'. What evidence in the portrait confirms this?
7. Look at Henry's calf muscles. Is this evidence of a lazy or active man?

Photos could be used to compare different kinds of 'portraits'.

Fact file

Parents	Henry VII and Elizabeth of York
Born	1491 at Greenwich
Reigned	1509 to 1547
Married	see page 7
Children	Mary I (Catherine of Aragon)
	Elizabeth I (Anne Boleyn)
	Edward VI (Jane Seymour)
Died	1547
Buried	St George's Chapel, Windsor

PHOTOPACK – *Tudor Monarchs*

© Folens

HAMPTON COURT

© Zefa Pictures

Built near the River Thames in Surrey, Hampton Court is one of the finest Renaissance palaces in Britain. Construction was begun by Cardinal Wolsey, Henry VIII's Lord Chancellor, who intended it to be his second palace. Wolsey built the Outer Court and the Fountain Court, while Henry VIII later added a new and larger Great Hall, the King's and Queen's Lodgings and chambers for courtiers. The Chapel was also remodelled by Henry.

Wolsey had a large moat dug around the palace. Like many contemporary palaces, Hampton Court was built on the river for ease of communication. River travel was quicker, easier and more comfortable than road travel. Henry added a tilt yard where he could enjoy horse riding and jousting. Hampton Court also had ponds, orchards, a bowling alley and a tennis court.

Henry's building programme was enormous. Not only were palaces constructed, but artists and craftspeople from all over Europe were brought to furnish and decorate the palaces. Wolsey and Henry were great patrons of the arts and the Tudors competed with the great dynasties of Europe in terms of artistic prestige.

Activities

- Using the activity sheet on page 14, ask the children to:
  - list ten rooms and describe the activities that took place there
  - sort the rooms into those where food was prepared and those where it was stored
  - decide which room was used for preparing poultry using boiling water.
- Baking and preparing poultry were the most dangerous jobs to be done in the kitchen. Ask the children what they notice about the plans of Hampton Court with regard to these jobs.
- Ask the children to investigate other issues, such as what people might have eaten and what kind of fuel might have been used.

Room	Preparation	Storage
Kitchen	✓	
Scalding house	✓	
Beer cellar		✓

Baking and preparing poultry were dangerous jobs.

Key questions

1. What building materials were used?
2. How many storeys are there in the tallest parts of the palace?
3. What can you see in the grounds?
4. Why would they plant lots of different trees?
5. Why was the palace built next to the river?
6. What are the advantages of having courtyards built in the centre of the palace?

Fact file

Built	Begun 1515
Original owner	Cardinal Wolsey
Later owner	Henry VIII
Location	On the River Thames, Surrey

THE FIELD OF THE CLOTH OF GOLD

The Royal Collection © Her Majesty the Queen

Much of Henry VIII's reign was characterised by foreign adventures that cost a great deal and achieved very little. In 1519 King Charles I of Spain succeeded his grandfather as Holy Roman Emperor, uniting two powerful empires.

Such a shift in the balance of power led Henry's chancellor, Cardinal Wolsey, to propose an alliance with France. A meeting was arranged in 1520 at Guisnes, just outside Calais, between Henry and Francis I of France. The venue became known as 'The Field of the Cloth of Gold' because of the sumptuous nature of both kings' tents. The two monarchs tried to outdo one another in the magnificence of their courts.

A particular feature of the 'Field' was a temporary palace constructed for Henry by Wolsey. The palace was the third largest building constructed during the early part of Henry's reign. The construction of the palace was later used against Wolsey when he faced charges of wasting money.

The A2 poster shows the temporary palace and the 'Field'. The perspective is clearly wrong but the elements are consistent with contemporary accounts. The A4 photo highlights the temporary palace.

H·R

The Tudor Royal Arms

- Ask the children to look closely at the poster and identify the banners of Henry and Francis. They could find out which banners are still used in England and France today.
- The children could research the cost and use of glass in Tudor times. Using their findings, encourage them to draw some conclusions about the cost of the temporary palace.

A nobleman

A servant woman

THE FAMILY OF HENRY VIII

The Royal
Collection
© Her Majesty
the Queen

The painting shows the family of Henry VIII by an unknown artist. It dates from about 1545 and shows Henry with his heir Edward VI to his right and Jane Seymour (Edward's mother) to his left. The future queens Mary and Elizabeth are also shown (Mary to his right and Elizabeth to his left).

Jane Seymour died in 1537, two weeks after the birth of Edward. When this picture was painted in 1545 Henry was actually married to Catherine Parr, so we can only speculate on why Jane Seymour appears in this painting with her eight-year-old son. It may well be that in giving birth to Henry's heir she was more highly regarded than any of his other wives. In fact, she shares Henry's tomb at Windsor. Romantics may prefer to believe that he loved her more than the rest, cynics may say that he would hardly have had time to tire of her.

The painting is from the ground floor of the King's lodgings at Whitehall Palace in London.

Activities

- Discuss with the children which character in the painting is the youngest and why he appears to be the most important child. A class discussion could include opinions about primogeniture and whether the children know that it still applies to the British aristocracy today.
- Ask the children to look carefully at the designs used in the coat of arms, embroidered canopy, carpet, ceiling, pillars and walls. They could design their own coat of arms, including events and symbols from their own family history or name.

Key questions

1. Who are the people in the painting?
2. What do you notice about the dresses the three women are wearing?
3. If the portrait shows Jane Seymour and Prince Edward, how do we know it was not painted from life?
4. Why would Henry want a painting to include his dead wife?
5. How might Catherine Parr have felt about this painting?
6. Which of the children does Henry appear to value most? How can you tell? Why do think this was?

Fact file

Catherine of Aragon

Anne Boleyn

Jane Seymour

Anne of Cleves

Catherine Howard

Catherine Parr

The Wives of Henry VIII

Year	Wife	Fate
1509	Catherine of Aragon	annulled 1533
1533	Anne Boleyn	executed 1536
1536	Jane Seymour	died 1537
1540	Anne of Cleves	annulled 1540
1540	Catherine Howard	executed 1542
1543	Catherine Parr	widowed 1547

EDWARD VI

By courtesy of the National Portrait Gallery, London

Edward was a sickly child, although relatively little is known about him. To some degree he was eclipsed by powerful magnates.

As Edward was only nine years old when he came to the throne, his uncle the Earl of Hertford (later Duke of Somerset) governed as 'Protector'. He was replaced by the Earl of Warwick (later Duke of Northumberland) in 1550. Edward's reign was marked by developments in Protestant supremacy. Both powerful earls favoured Protestanism and Edward probably supported it.

The painting shows Edward at about the time of his accession. The pose is very similar to that adopted by his father and made famous by Holbein. The proportions appear strange because Edward's clothes have been filled out to give him an appearance closer to that of Henry VIII. However, his relatively thin legs and face appear at odds with the large torso. The whiteness of his face is more likely to reflect fashion than illness – white lead-based make-up was used by men and women. A pale complexion was desirable because it implied a lack of time spent outdoors. This in turn implied a higher social position, because tanned skin was the result of manual labour.

Activities

- Ask the children to compare this painting with that of Henry VIII. They could describe any similarities or differences.

Feature	Henry VIII	Edward VI
Posture		
Legs		
Dress		
Ornament		
Weapon		
Physical resemblance		
Floor		

- The children could paint themselves as smaller versions of their parents, just as this artist did when painting Edward.

Key questions

1. How old do you think Edward looks?
2. What evidence is there that he is a king?
3. Who does his pose remind you of?
4. How do the surroundings make him look important?
5. Which of the following words best describe Edward in the painting? *strong, weak, confident, healthy, sickly, poor, wealthy, firm, gentle, frightened, proud, snooty.*

The Duke of Somerset, the first 'Protector' of Edward VI.

Fact file

Parents	Henry VIII and Jane Seymour
Born	1537 at Hampton Court
Reigned	1547 to 1553 (aged 9 to 15)
Married	No
Children	None
Died	1553
Buried	Westminster Abbey

PHOTOPACK – *Tudor Monarchs*

© Folens

LADY JANE GREY

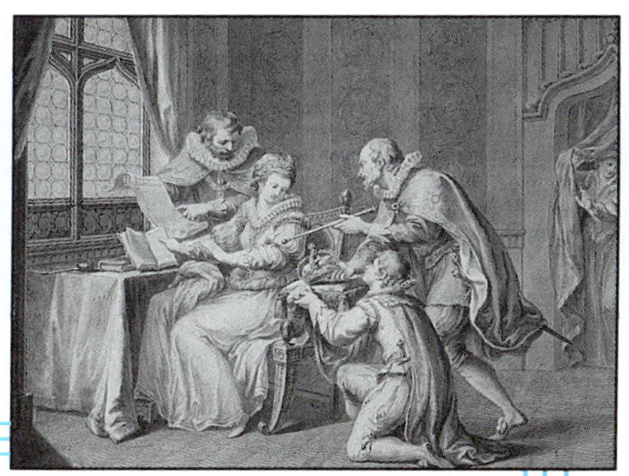

© Victoria and Albert Museum /
Bridgeman Art Library, London

As Edward VI lay dying, power rested with the Duke of Northumberland. He persuaded Edward that the rightful heir to the throne was Lady Jane Grey. She was a Protestant and the great niece of Henry VIII, but her claim to the throne was far inferior to that of Edward's half-sister, Princess Mary.

Northumberland kept news of Edward's death a secret while he planned for Lady Jane Grey's succession. Jane was Northumberland's daughter-in-law. It appears she did not actively seek the throne, but did as she was told by Northumberland and her father, the Duke of Suffolk.

Jane was proclaimed Queen on 10 July 1553. Northumberland then marched on Framlingham Castle where Mary was in residence, but the claim that Mary was illegitimate did not receive popular support. Northumberland's forces began to desert while supporters flocked to Mary. Lady Jane's father, Suffolk, abandoned his daughter. She was arrested and taken to the Tower of London along with her husband Lord Dudley. Dudley was executed first. Jane saw his headless body return before she too was beheaded.

Fact file

Parents	The Duke and Duchess of Suffolk
Born	1537 at Bradgate Park, Leicester
Reigned	1553 for nine days
Married	Lord Dudley
Children	None
Died	1554
Buried	Chapel of St Peter ad Vincula

Key questions

1. What is each person holding?
2. How is each man persuading Lady Jane to take the throne?
3. What do you think Lady Jane was doing before the men entered her room?
4. Who do you think are the women who are watching?
5. Do you think the men knew they were being watched?
6. Why might this worry them?
7. How old was Lady Jane when she was executed?
8. Do you think it was her idea to take the throne? Explain.
9. Look at Lady Jane's clothes. Are they similar to other women's in Tudor times?
10. This painting was produced in the eighteenth century, about 200 years after the event took place. Does this affect its value as historical evidence?

Lady Jane Grey ruled for only nine days in 1553.

Activities

- Imagine you were Lady Jane Grey. You have just seen your husband beheaded. How would you feel? What has happened? Why?
- Why do you think Dudley, Suffolk and Northumberland wanted Lady Jane to be queen? List what each person might have to gain or lose.

Person	If Lady Jane became queen	If Mary became queen
Lord Suffolk		
Duke of Northumberland		
Lady Jane Grey		
Lord Dudley		

MARY I

Mary I was Henry VIII's eldest child and daughter of his first wife. When Henry's marriage to Catherine of Aragon was annulled in 1533, Mary was declared illegitimate. She was a staunch Catholic and resisted pressure during her brother Edward's reign to convert to Protestantism. During her reign she tried to restore the Catholic religion.

Mary married King Philip of Spain in Winchester Cathedral in 1554. The marriage was meant to bring together two Catholic monarchs, but it proved to be an unsuccessful alliance. Philip probably disliked her because she appeared older than her years. He soon returned to Spain.

The marriage to a Catholic Spaniard alienated many people in England. In addition, Mary's obsession with restoring Catholicism in England led to religious persecution. Many people were burned at the stake. She became known as 'Bloody Mary'.

© Prado, Madrid / Scala, Florence

Activities

- Ask the children to compare this portrait to the painting of Mary as a young princess with the rest of her family. How has she changed?

Feature	Young princess	Queen
Face		
Jewellery		
Fashion		
Hairstyle		
Facial expression		

- The children could also compare the portrait of Mary I with the portrait of Elizabeth I (page 11). Factors to be compared could include symbols of monarchy, setting, ornateness, style and dress.

Feature	Elizabeth I	Mary I
Symbols of monarchy		
Dress		
Surroundings		

Key questions

1. Describe Mary. Are there any signs that she is a Tudor queen?
2. Which of the following words best fit the portrait? *kind, stubborn, friendly, spoilt, jolly, moody, impatient.*
3. What is she holding in her right hand? What is it a symbol of?
4. The pendant was a wedding gift from Philip of Spain. How do you think she felt when she received it?
5. What religious symbol is Mary wearing?
6. How many rings is she wearing?

Fact file

Parents	Henry VIII and Catherine of Aragon
Born	1516 at Greenwich Palace
Reigned	1553 to 1558
Married	Philip II of Spain
Children	None
Died	1558
Buried	Westminster Abbey

Throughout Tudor times, the red rose represented both the House of Tudor and love (see page 3).

ELIZABETH I

© Private Collection /
Bridgeman Art
Library, London

During the reign of Elizabeth I, the Protestant cause became dominant once more. Her personal beliefs had been questioned but she recognised the political reality that she should rule as a Protestant head of state. Relations with Spain (a Catholic country) were strained from early in her reign.

The Netherlands sought independence from Spain and looked to Elizabeth as a fellow Protestant who could save them. In 1570 Pope Pius VI invited Catholic princes to overthrow her. In 1584 she sent the Earl of Leicester to assist the Dutch in their war against Spain. Also, Francis Drake plundered the West Indies (Spanish possessions). In 1588 these events culminated in the Armada.

King Philip sent an Armada (a large fleet of about 150 ships) to meet his army in the Netherlands in order to carry them across the Channel to invade England. The English fleet battled with the Armada at Gravelines. Winds blew the Spanish fleet north, but they had no accurate charts. Some ships sank and others were captured by the Dutch. About half of the original fleet returned to Spain.

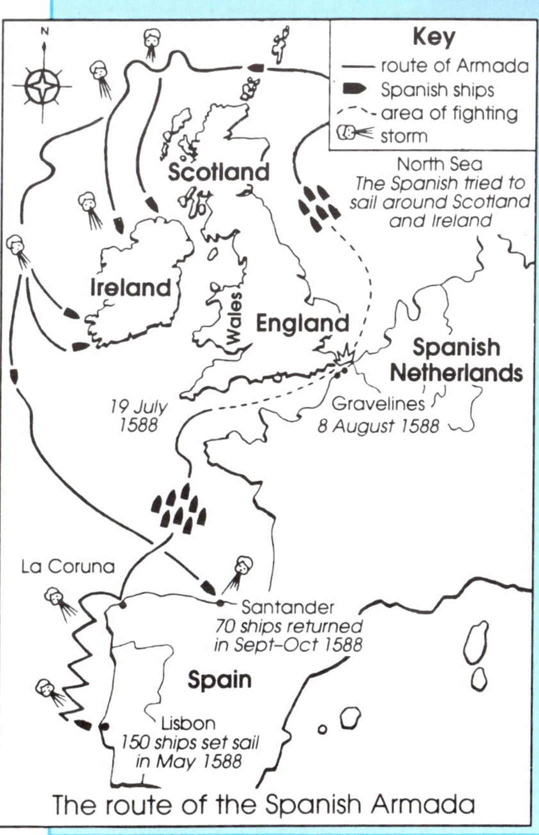

The route of the Spanish Armada

Activities

- Recount the story of the Armada and ask the children to use reference material to research dates and events in sequence. The route of the Armada could then be plotted on an outline map and dates placed on the map to indicate key events.
- Ask the children to imagine they were involved in the Armada and compile a ship's log of their adventures. They could decide whether to be a captain of a Spanish or an English ship. They could enter the dates and describe the events and their feelings.

Key questions

1. How do we know she is the queen?
2. Where and when does the portrait appear to have been painted?
3. Was Elizabeth actually present at the battle?
4. Do the two windows show the same event?
5. How and why are they different?
6. Is this a portrait of a victorious or a defeated queen? Explain.
7. Why does Elizabeth have her hand on a globe?

Fact file

Parents	Henry VIII and Anne Boleyn
Born	1533 at Greenwich Palace
Reigned	1558 to 1603
Married	No
Children	None
Died	1603
Buried	Westminster Abbey

MARY QUEEN OF SCOTS

© Scottish National Portrait Gallery

Mary Queen of Scots succeeded to the throne of Scotland in 1542 at the age of just six days. In 1543 she was betrothed to Henry VIII's son Edward, but conflict between England and Scotland led to her removal to France, where a Scottish-French treaty was agreed. In 1558 Mary Queen of Scots married Francis II of France. She had a clear claim to the English throne.

In 1560 Francis died. In 1561 Mary (a firm Catholic) returned to rule Scotland, which was turning to Protestantism. In 1565 Mary married Lord Darnley, a Catholic and great-grandson of Henry VIII. A year later Mary gave birth to the future James VI of Scotland.

Following a scandal surrounding the murder of Darnley, Mary was imprisoned. She abdicated the Scottish throne in favour of her son James and escaped from prison. She fled to England, hoping for mercy from Elizabeth, but spent the next 17 years in prison. In 1586 there was an alleged plot to free Mary and kill Elizabeth. Mary was charged with treason and executed in February 1587. Three strokes of the axe were needed to remove her head.

Fact file

Parents	James V of Scotland and Mary of Guise (French)
Born	1542
Reigned	1542 to 1567 in Scotland (from France through a regent until 1561)
Married	1. 1558 King Francis II of France, died 1560
	2. 1565 Lord Darnley, murdered 1567
	3. 1567 Lord Bothwell
Children	James VI of Scotland, later James I of England
Died	1587 executed at Fotheringhay Castle

Key questions

1. How was Mary executed?
2. Do you think the executioner was a popular man?
3. The person being executed often gave the executioner some money. Why do you think this might be? (This was to encourage an accurate first chop, as sometimes the first blow was not always fatal.)
4. Who do you think the two ladies were? How do you think they felt about the execution?
5. What is the book beside Mary? (It is a Bible.)
6. Who are the most important men? (The two sitting down.)
7. What is the man in the foreground doing? (The Dean of Peterborough, asking her to renounce her faith. He failed!)
8. What do you think is being burned?

Activities

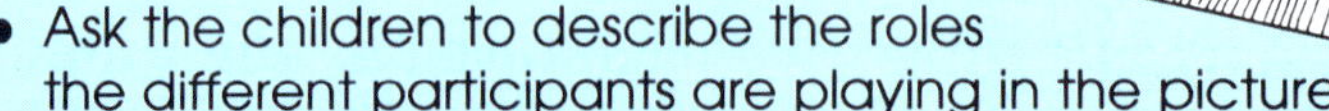

An execution block and axe.

- Ask the children to describe the roles the different participants are playing in the picture.
- Show the children a copy of part of the family tree (page 13) that shows how Mary and Elizabeth were related. Explain that Elizabeth had no children. Ask them to think of possible reasons why Elizabeth should or should not execute Mary.
- This is a Dutch painting. Ask the children to examine it closely and answer some questions, such as:
  – Why were the Dutch interested in events in England?
  – How well did the Dutch artist represent the English?
  – How would the artist know what happened? Would he have been there with his easel?
- The children could look at other contemporary pictures showing how people dressed in Tudor times.

THE TUDOR FAMILY TREE

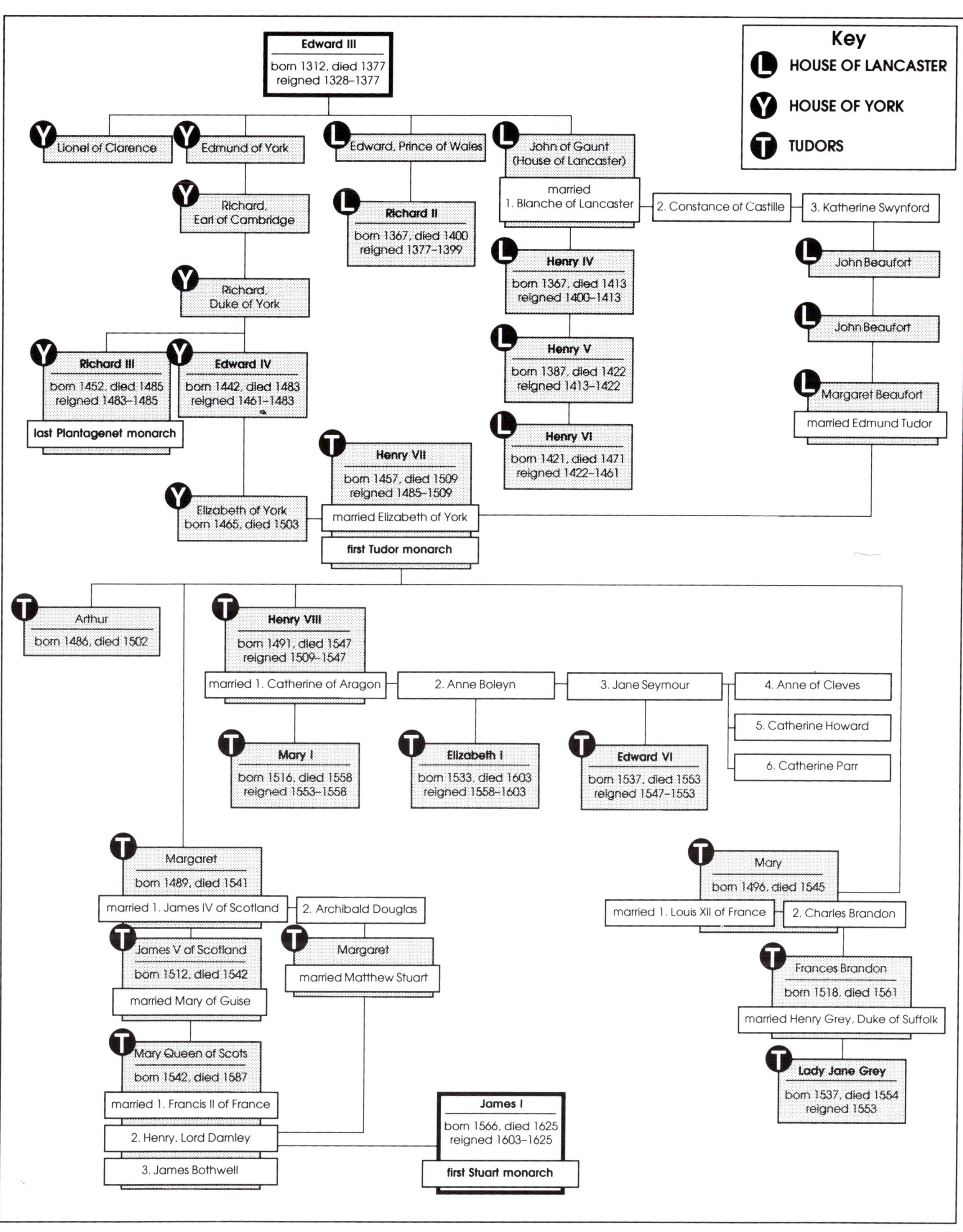

HAMPTON COURT KITCHENS

Ground floor plan of the kitchens.

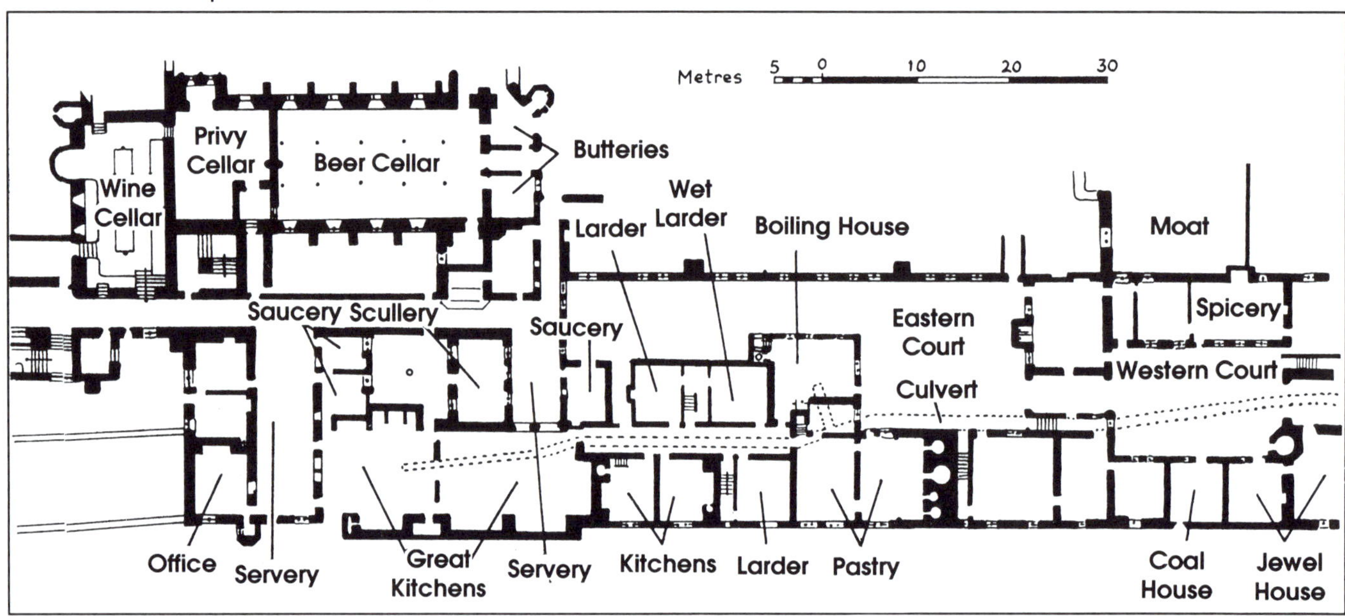

Plan of the houses and offices.

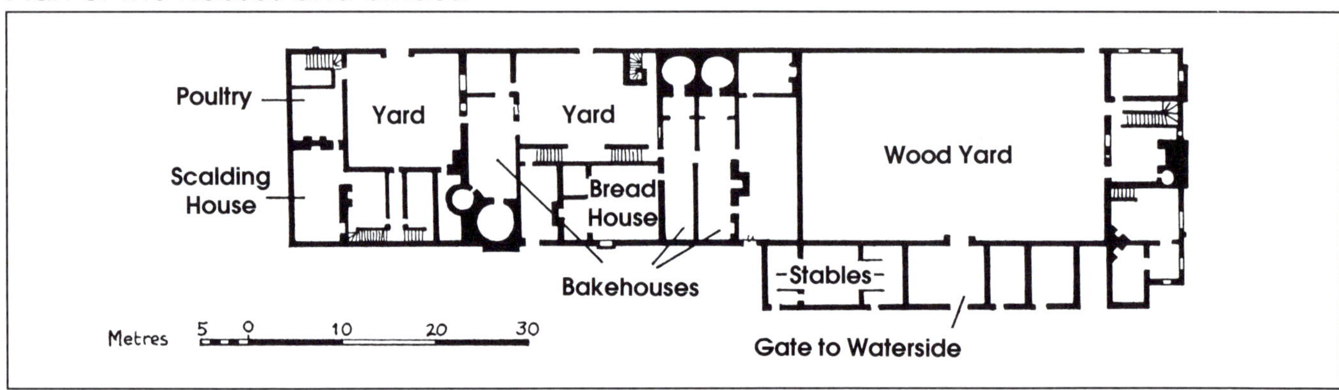

Look at both plans.

1. Do you think large numbers of people were entertained here? Explain your answer.
2. What did they drink with their meals?
3. What kind of food was cooked?
4. Rooms where fire was a hazard were often separated from other rooms. Write a list of the rooms where fire was used and say what you think happened in each room.
5. Draw and complete a chart like this to show what activity took place in each room.

Room	Activity
scalding house	

    PHOTOPACK – *Tudor Monarchs*   © Folens (copiable page)

THE TUDOR MONARCH FACT FILE

Henry VII

Parents	Edmund Tudor and Margaret Beaufort
Born	1457 at Pembroke Castle
Reigned	1485 to 1509
Married	Elizabeth of York
Children	Arthur, Henry VIII, Margaret, Mary
Died	1509
Buried	Westminster Abbey

Henry VIII

Parents	Henry VII and Elizabeth of York
Born	1491 at Greenwich
Reigned	1509 to 1547
Married	Catherine of Aragon, Anne Boleyn, Jane Seymour, Anne of Cleves, Catherine Howard, Catherine Parr
Children	Mary I, Elizabeth I, Edward VI
Died	1547
Buried	St George's Chapel, Windsor

Mary I

Parents	Henry VIII and Catherine of Aragon
Born	1516 at Greenwich Palace
Reigned	1553 to 1558
Married	Philip II of Spain
Children	None
Died	1558
Buried	Westminster Abbey

Elizabeth I

Parents	Henry VIII and Anne Boleyn
Born	1533 at Greenwich Palace
Reigned	1558 to 1603
Married	No
Children	None
Died	1603
Buried	Westminster Abbey

Edward VI

Parents	Henry VIII and Jane Seymour
Born	1537 at Hampton Court
Reigned	1547 to 1553 (aged 9 to 15 years)
Married	No
Children	None
Died	1553
Buried	Westminster Abbey

WHO AM I?

Who am I?

- My father was Henry VIII.
- I reigned for five years.

Answer – Mary I

Who am I?

- I became queen when I was 25 years old.
- I never married.

Answer – Elizabeth I

Who am I?

- My wife was Elizabeth of York.
- I was born in 1457.

Answer – Henry VII

Who am I?

- I was born in 1491.
- All three of my children became monarchs.

Answer – Henry VIII

Who am I?

- I reigned for six years.
- My father was Henry VIII.

Answer – Edward VI

Who am I?

- My grandfather was Henry VII.
- I had two half-sisters.

Answer – Edward VI

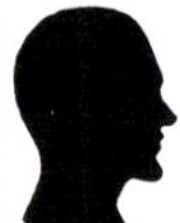

Who am I?

- My elder brother died before my father.
- I reigned for 38 years.

Answer – Henry VIII

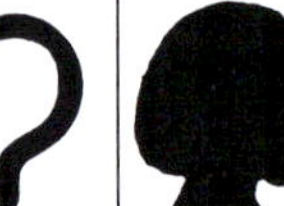

Who am I?

- I was born in the sixteenth century.
- I died in the seventeenth century.

Answer – Elizabeth I

Who am I?

- My grandfather had four children.
- My sister was born when I was 17 years old.

Answer – Mary I

Teacher's notes (delete before copying).

- Enlarge this sheet to A3, copy on to card, cut out each individual card and laminate.
- Give the children a copy of page 13 (the Tudor family tree) and page 15 (the Tudor monarch fact file).
- Working in pairs, the children could play this game as a quiz. They could use the family tree and the fact file to work out the answers.
- They could work out how they will score. They could introduce a time factor, for example:
  - the correct answer in 30 seconds gives 5 points
  - the correct answer in 1 minute gives 3 points, and so on.

   PHOTOPACK – *Tudor Monarchs*   © Folens (copiable page)